My Journey For GOD'S GLORY

MICHELE THOMPSON-GRANT

Editing, cover and author services by Opulent Books www.OpulentBooks.net

ISBN: 978-1-916691-34-6

Acknowledgments

To Flavius Grant my Husband

My greatest cheerleader, thank you for sticking with me through thick and thin. You are indeed a Man of God, a special human being, your integrity, and character are very admirable. You are full of wisdom and very knowledgeable, yet so humble. I love you, babes.

Dr. Augustine Odih

Pastor/Director of Programs – Deeper Life School of Evangelism. Dr. Odih, thanks for the special emphasis you place on studying the Word of God and Prayer. This has left an indelible mark on my life and it was one of the best decisions I made in my entire life. You are a walking, talking Bible you epitomize humility which is rare in today's society. I salute you, Sir!

Table of Contents

Preface

In pursuing one's purpose in life, many individuals embark on transformative journeys that lead them toward a higher vocation seeking a connection with God. Such a journey often unfolds as a quest for God's glory – a path illuminated by faith, soul searching, and spiritual growth. This preface examines the personal expedition of one such seeker, navigating the intricacies of life in a deeper understanding of the Divine, and a desire to contribute to the Glory of God.

"*My Journey for God's Glory*" is an intimate exploration, a sojourn into the realms of faith, reflection, and self-realization. It is a narrative shaped by moments of profound revelation, challenges that test the spirit, and encounters that redefine one's relationship with God. Through this prelude, I invite readers to accompany me on a heartfelt expedition, discovering the twists and turns of my spiritual path.

The narration unfolds against the backdrop of the human experience, where the everyday and the extraordinary coverage. From the mundane struggles of daily life to the next exceptional moments of Divine intervention, the seeker's journey is marked by a patchwork of emotions, lessons, and experiences. It is a story of perseverance, resilience, and unwavering faith, a testament to the transformational power of God in shaping one's character and purpose.

As I share my reflections on the milestones and

challenges I met on this spiritual pilgrimage, you are invited to contemplate your journey. It is a universal exposition that transcends cultural and religious boundaries emphasizing the common threads that bind humanity in its mission for meaning and connection with the Lord.

This opening set the stage for an account that seeks to inspire, encourage, and provoke consideration. It is an invitation to explore the depths of spirituality, grapple with the questions that define the human experience, and celebrate the moments of Divine grace that brighten the pathway toward God's glory. As we embark on this literary journey, may the words resonate with you, offering insights solace, and a shared sense of purpose in the pursuit of something greater than ourselves.

Introduction

I am absolutely thrilled to celebrate the release of my first book, *"My Journey for God's Glory."* Such an opportunity has filled me with immense joy. This is a dream come true for me, and I am eternally grateful to Almighty God for the vision, potential, and ability to write this book, and, most importantly, to the Holy Spirit—the Comforter that abides in me.

I want to share a prophecy the Lord gave me, which I journaled on June 20, 2022. I believe it is very appropriate at this time: **"I handpicked you, ordained, orchestrated you for this time. You**

will achieve much more than past generations. You will succeed and launch out into the deep. I will never fail you; your purpose cannot die, and you were handpicked for this."

I knew God chose me to change my family tree—from prayer meetings on the mountain to country areas and family prayer at home with my husband and his sister. I was chosen from the foundation of the earth, a little girl hurt by the people she loved and trusted. Yet, God, in His infinite mercy, rearranged my life. He delivered, saved, and set me apart for His glory. I can relate to the Prophet Isaiah in Chapter 61:1 (KJV): "*The spirit of the Lord God is upon me, because the Lord hath anointed me to preach good tidings unto the meek; he hath sent me to bind up the brokenhearted, to proclaim liberty to the captives, and the opening of the prison to them that are bound.*" I was chosen by God to be afflicted so I could bring the Good News of Jesus.

One might assume that my benevolence stems from an easy life, but they don't know the depth of my journey through the valley of the shadow of death. The transforming power of God has turned my pain into power, wounds into wisdom, mistreatment into boundaries, and now I walk in God's original design.

Transitioning from traumas to freedom, from pain to peace, from indecision to action, from confusion to clarity, from frustration to anticipation, from being overwhelmed to being set free, from fear to courage, from suppressing issues to having the tenacity to face them—from numbing thoughts to capturing them, from passivity to passion, from being a late bloomer to being successful.

Regardless of what I've been through, I remain

sensitive to the needs of others, believing everyone can win. I am an encourager and a giver; people are drawn to me because I am easy to talk to and a good listener. I am not prejudiced, and I detest injustice. I am unafraid to get my hands dirty to proclaim the Gospel of Jesus Christ.

Ready to share my experiences, I aim to help boys, girls, men, and women who may have gone through situations described in this book. To the boys who feel isolated due to the family they were born into and the young lady struggling with low self-esteem because her mother is dismissive—I want to convey that Jesus is the answer. I encourage them not to let negative thoughts take root, to forgive quickly, as sin is the reason bad things happen to good people. Yet, we are overcomers through the finished work of Jesus Christ—all our sins are nailed to the cross. So, we can rejoice in hope. To God be the glory for the things He has done.

CHAPTER 1

Forgiveness is Divine

To err is human, but to forgive is Divine. There were times in my life when forgiveness was not my ideal cup of tea. I struggled with unforgiveness. If anyone wronged or offended me, vexation would set in, leading me to cut them off completely and hold a grudge for a very long time. Looking back now, if God were like man, I would have been consumed.

Amazing Grace, how sweet the sound, that saved a wretch like me! I once was lost, but now am found; was blind, but now I see. Growing up, I didn't know any better; I had been surrounded by a mindset where cutting ties and holding grudges were the norm—whether it was with our neighbors, peers, or even some family members who have since passed without making restitution.

I have encountered situations where I was deeply hurt by the actions of others. My initial reaction was often anger and a desire for revenge, but I soon realized that holding onto these negative emotions only perpetuated my suffering. It was as if I was carrying a heavy load of negativity that weighed me down and prevented me from moving forward in life.

Through introspection, self-discovery, and salvation, I began to see that forgiveness was a way to set myself free. It allowed me to let go of the past pain associated with it—a very liberating experience to release the chains that bound me to hurtful memories, to stop dwelling on what had been done to me, and to focus on my healing and growth.

I have found forgiveness to be a gift to myself, and as I practice forgiveness, I have discovered great peace that I had not experienced before, confronting the idea of justice. Forgiveness, for me, is not a one-size-fits-all solution. The process was not easy, taking years to rid myself of unforgiving feelings, while for others, it may happen quickly. Sometimes, seeking closure through communication with the wrongdoer may never happen; it could be an entirely internal process where you release your emotional attachment to the hurt. Mark Twain's quote resonates with me: "Forgiveness is the fragrance that the violet sheds on the heel that has crushed it."

True forgiveness means giving up any claim you have against another person for an offense they have committed—an act of granting full pardon without harboring any resentment towards the offender. Whether it is a close friend, a family member, a colleague, or even yourself, if you believe you have forgiven someone and still feel uneasy toward them at times, you need to ask God to show you just how true your forgiveness is.

It is a complex and deeply personal process that involves both the mind and the heart. Forgiveness is a conscious choice to move forward and heal from the pain, restoring a sense of emotional well-being. Moreover, forgiveness can lead to reconciliation and pave the way for rebuilding relationships and bridges that were burned beyond repair, offering an opportunity for both parties to grow from their past mistakes. Forgiveness is a powerful tool that I have learned to wield. It is a choice I make, not for the benefit of those who have wronged me, but for my own good.

Forgiveness is a profound act of compassion and liberation—a process that allows individuals to break free from the shackles of the enemy and bring healing and restoration to the forgiver. By choosing forgiveness, all parties win, fostering a healthier relationship, cultivating empathy, and embarking on a path of inner peace. Forgiveness is not an exception; it is the rule. There are no unforgiving people in the Kingdom of God.

Let's explore in the scriptures the Divine nature of forgiveness. It's not just an unforgiving spirit that separates a person from God; it is sin, as mentioned in Matthew 5:29a (ESV), "*If your right eye causes you to sin, tear it out and throw it away.*" Many Christians still grapple with forgiving others, though they may not admit it, often due to ego. Everyone contends with unforgiveness at various points in their lifetime. Sometimes, the hurt or scar runs so deep, and you might find yourself saying, "I gave them the best years of my life," or "I have done so much for this person, and what they did to me is unforgivable."

Forgiveness is a matter that must be settled here on earth. The Bible speaks extensively about forgiveness in Matthew 6:12 (KJV), *"Forgive us our debts, as we forgive our debtors."* When strongholds are involved, forgiveness can be very challenging (see St. Mark 11:25). Forgiving unconditionally brings incredible rewards that cannot be obtained in any other way. A forgiving person experiences total freedom from responding to, reacting to, and replaying past hurts.

Don't curse it. When you are hurt, resist the urge to retaliate, take revenge, or strike back. Leave the offense in God's hands. Romans 12:19 (KJV) counsels, "*Dearly beloved, avenge not yourselves, but rather give place unto God's wrath, for it is written: Vengeance is Mine, I will repay, says the Lord.*"

Don't rehearse it. Resentment is addictive and is the greatest killer of relationships. It causes you to focus only on the past, diverting attention from the present and the future. Job 5:2 warns that you can become addicted to the feeling of resentment if you rehearse it, so guard against it before it destroys you.

Don't nurse it. If you are angry, avoid sinning by nursing your grudge (Ephesians 4:26-27). While anger is a fair response to disappointment and hurt, it becomes dangerous when you stay angry for an extended period and nurse the grudge. This opens the door for Satan to torment you and keeps you trapped in unforgiveness and bitterness. Get angry, if you need to, but also get over it quickly. Pray for

God's help, forget the hurt, and release any resentment you may have toward others, trusting that He will bring justice in His perfect timing.

Disperse it. Lift your hurts, anger, and frustration to God in prayer. Let them go; don't hold onto them. When you give your pain to the Lord, something wonderful happens—God helps you forget the pain, sorrows, and grievances you've experienced (Genesis 41:50-51). The key to forgiveness is forgetfulness, and this is how God forgives us—by forgetting the wrongs we have done.

Let God Reverse it. You may wonder about the evildoers who have hurt you. Psalm 37:1-2 provides clarity: "*Fret not thyself because of evildoers, neither be thou envious against the workers of iniquity; for they shall soon be cut down like the grass and wither as the green herbs.*" God will correct every wrong and deal with all evildoers in time. Leave everything to God and let Him be the Judge.

Consider how Jesus dealt with forgiveness in the Gospel of St. Luke 23:34-37 (KJV). We witness this when Jesus was being nailed to the cross, enduring unthinkable actions from his accusers. His response was astounding—He prayed to God, saying, *"Forgive them, for they know not what they do."*

However, in today's environment, the concept of forgiveness seems foreign. People may not only hold grudges against those who have wronged them individually but also against entire groups of people, often feeling justified in their anger. Seeking payback and suffering for wrongdoing have become commonplace in the world system. The desire for revenge, going beyond an eye for an eye, has taken root in society, and the entertainment industry knows how to capitalize on this theme, constantly portraying it in movies.

Contrary to this prevailing sentiment, Jesus teaches us to approach things differently. Instead of seeking retaliation and speaking evil about those who wrong us, He instructs us in St. Matthew 5:43-45 to forgive, love, and overlook wrongdoing. Jesus understands that the motivations of people are rooted in the unseen realm, as described in Ephesians 6:12-13 (KJV):

"For we wrestle not against flesh and blood, but against principalities, against powers, against the rulers of the darkness of this world, against spiritual wickedness in high places." These are powerful demonic forces influencing the world, and many times, they work through people.

Therefore, if you encounter trouble in one area with certain people, failing to forgive and walk in love may allow that same spirit to manifest through interactions with others wherever you go. To defeat this spirit, you must stand in faith, obey the commandment of love, and take authority over it through prayer. Pray with compassion for the person through whom that spirit is manifesting because they are being used by it.

This spirit operates initially through the thought life. Many believers fail to discern thought lives and may adopt wrong thinking as their own, instead of following the Word of God, which instructs them to cast down imaginations that exalt themselves against the knowledge of God. Rather than meditating on negative thoughts, believers should take authority over them, preventing them from turning into emotions, verbalizations, and actions.

Once we realize that not every thought is our own, we can then exercise more power and authority over them. Many thoughts come from the Holy Spirit, while others come from the enemy. We must discern closely whether the thoughts align with God's word or not. If they do not, then we are to cast them down. We are to "take no thought of it."

Just imagine if every believer you know obeyed the commandment of love to treat others the way they want to be treated! 1 Corinthians 13 will significantly help you love each other more. Read it, meditate on it, memorize it, live it, and walk in love. Instantaneous unity in the church and world would result, and all strife and division would be defeated. However, we are not there yet. Therefore, choose to walk in love regardless of what others are doing around you; love never fails.

When you walk in love, there will be no occasion of stumbling, and your faith will always work (1 Peter 3:9-11 AMP). Never return evil for evil; hard times and painful experiences do happen to Christians. But these times do not have to be endured; going through trials with the right attitude can become an experience and hope in our soul (Romans 5:3-4). The word "experience" in verse 4 means acceptable, proven, tried, and trusted; in other words, it is you.

During our Christian journey, our watchword should always be forgiveness. It doesn't matter who has hurt you; choose to forgive. Ask God to forgive you for any wrong pattern of thinking. Indeed, He is the master of forgiveness. Learn from Him how to forgive even when people are not sorry. Pray to loosen all opposition, rigidity, and entrenched stubbornness from our souls. Let us be patient with each other and help us grow into the spiritual experience and be overcomers. Amen!

CHAPTER 2

God Made You Special

Before starting this chapter, I went through a process of decluttering papers and was pleasantly surprised by my findings. Two greeting cards caught my attention—one from my mother for my birthday and the other from a church sister whom I had blessed with a gift a few years ago. As I reread the first part of the card from Mom, it read, "From the very first day you were born, it was clear there was something special about you that would make others always want to have you near. It's a feeling that grows right along with you." I got all teary and felt so special.

The other card was beautifully handmade and decorated by this person. It read, "I wish I had time to tell you how God used your gifts in a train of events to teach me and to encourage me. Truly, I am continually amazed at God's mysterious and dumbfounding ways. As a matter of fact, it was part of the 'testimony' I shared with my hairdresser. Thanks for your love and thanks for sharing God's love with me. It's a blessed ministry."

I didn't always feel special in my formative years and early adulthood. I was repeatedly told, even by some of my relatives, that I would not amount to anything. I believed all these verbal abuses and disadvantages as a child.

My mother took me to the country to live in the rural part of St. Elizabeth with my grandparents and aunt. She had to work in the city, and no one was there to take care of me. She did her very best to provide me with everything I needed. She was a good, calm, and strong mother, a peacemaker, and I emulate some of these qualities. However, I needed her as a child, and my experience in the country was very devastating.

My aunt was in a very abusive relationship, and I was with her most of the time. She took out most of her frustration on me. Also, she and my mother didn't get along. I did not know the full story of the sibling rivalry between my mother and aunt until it was revealed by my cousin after the death of my mother.

Growing up, I got the hard end of the stick, but "Still I Rise," and I am reminded of Jeremiah 29:11 (KJV), *"For I know the thoughts that I think toward you, says the Lord, thoughts of peace and not of evil, to give you an expected end."* This means I am not free from facing difficult situations, and it is not a promise to be immediately rescued from hardship or suffering. Instead, God has a plan for my life irrespective of what has happened in the past or my current situation. He can work through it to prosper me and give me hope.

In 1993, I went through a failed relationship, a terrible breakup, and I was a mess. However, God intervened. I felt like I couldn't take life anymore. My life changed dramatically when my mother and I were invited to a gospel crusade by her co-worker in November 1993. I accepted Jesus Christ as my personal Savior, and on the last day of December of the same year, I rang in the new year of 1994, submerged under water, and started walking with Jesus. I must confess I've fallen down many times, but I get up, brush myself off, and begin again because of my true convictions and the Holy Spirit that lives in me.

The inspiration for this topic is quite ironic; it was one of those moments when discouragement slipped in, and I questioned the Lord, Why? I was dealing with a particular issue and not seeing the light at the end of the tunnel. That's when I heard, in an audible voice, the phrase "God made you special." Knowing me, I don't take things at face value, so I immediately delved into my regular devotion and reflections. This study was mind-blowing, and I also heard that it was time to write that book, so I started immediately.

Have you ever heard anyone say, "God made you special"? When those words are uttered, it draws internal queries from most, even those who are blessed with supernatural abilities and talents to do great exploits. Funnily, the term "God made you special" seems like a cliché.

It appears meaningless for the majority of us, which prompts the question: were we made special? It seems absurd to think that one born with disabilities is special, but yes, we were all created special in the image and likeness of God. We are special because there are no two of us; each of us is singular in our makeup. There is something you can do that only you can do better than anyone else.

We all view things differently, even if we share the same environment, are educated to the same level, and have similar likenesses and shared experiences. Our peculiar existence is mysterious and obvious in our daily actions. People with similar blood types do not share the same career goals and have different aspirations. Where did this come from? It came from the creator. He is the master designer of all life forms.

Our uniqueness exposes the greatness of our

God and confounds the wisdom of man. We are special when we see ourselves created in the likeness and image of God. This thought may be hard to fathom, but it gives us confidence in whatever we set out to do.

It is because we are special that our gifting differs. Looking at the Bible's perspective, the concept that God made each individual special is rooted in the belief that God is the creator of all things, including human beings made in the image of God (Genesis 1:27). This permeates each person with inherent dignity, worth, and uniqueness.

Here are some key biblical passages that highlight the idea that God made you special:

1. **Psalm 139:13-14:** *"For you formed my inward parts; you knitted me together in my mother's womb. I praise you, for I am fearfully and wonderfully made. Wonderful are your*

works; my soul knows it very well." This verse emphasizes that God personally crafts each individual, and their creation is a marvelous work of God's hand.

2. **Ephesians 2:10:** "*For we are his workmanship, created in Christ Jesus for good works, which God prepared beforehand that we should walk in them.*" This highlights that believers are God's handiwork, created with a purpose for good works. Each person has unique talents, abilities, and gifts bestowed upon them by God.

3. **Jeremiah 1:5:** "*Before I formed you in the womb, I knew you; before you were born, I set you apart; I appointed you as a prophet to the nations.*" This passage shows that God has a plan and purpose for each person even before they are born. It underscores the

special calling and uniqueness of individuals in fulfilling God's purposes.

In essence, God intentionally creates each person, endowing them with individuality, purpose, and value. Each person is considered special and unique in God's sight, and their life has meaning and significance within God's Divine plan. God wants each of us to become the person He made us to be, living life well and displaying his splendor and glory! While the phrase "God made you special" may sound overused, it is nevertheless true.

The expression "God made you special" can also serve as a reminder to treat oneself and others with kindness, compassion, and respect, recognizing that everyone has inherent worth and dignity. Additionally, this concept can inspire individuals to embrace their individuality, talents, and strengths, recognizing that these qualities were given to them for a reason and can be used to make a positive impact in the world.

CHAPTER 3

My Path to Freedom and Redemption: Breaking Generational Curses

---

In the heart of a small, unassuming countryside, the roots of my family's history ran deep—a place where secrets were whispered from one generation to the next, continuing a cycle of pain and suffering that seemed impossible to escape. From a tender age, I felt the weight of these chains, unaware of the legacy they carried and the profound impact they would have on my life.

The story of my generation was etched into the very fabric of our existence and passed down like a birthright. Struggles and mistakes echoed through the years, leaving an indelible mark on the lives of those who followed.

As a child, I couldn't comprehend the details of generational curses, but I could sense the palpable tension lingering in our home. My extended family, carrying their own burdens from the past, fought silent battles that played out before my innocent eyes. I longed for a sense of normalcy, an escape from the shadows threatening to engulf me.

As I grew older in my Christian journey, the pattern became clearer. I noticed striking resemblances between my life and my extended family's. It was as if destiny had scripted a predetermined path, and we were mere actors reciting lines spoken countless times before.

The realization that I was following in their footsteps filled me with dread. I didn't want to repeat the same mistakes or endure the same pain, yet the invisible hand of the past seemed to guide my actions, nudging me toward a fate I desperately wished to avoid. With each passing year, the weight of my family history grew heavier.

Determined by the help of God to break off these surmountable mountains blocking my path to freedom and redemption, I yearned to break free from the confines of this generational curses prison. The task seemed daunting and overwhelming, especially after my mother passed in February 2022, leading me to extensive study on the topic. I wanted to understand so I could pray accordingly.

But in the midst of darkness, a glimmer of hope emerged. Guided by God and the power of the Holy Spirit, the word of God, and prayer, I had the power to change the narrative, to alter the course of my life, and to sever the chains that bound me. The courage to challenge the status quo blossomed within me, and I decided to embark on a path of restoration.

I sought wisdom from those who had walked similar paths, and transformative books became my companions, offering insights and guidance on breaking free from generational curses. Eager to learn from experts who could illuminate the way forward, my journey was not without challenges. I confronted painful memories and emotions that I had suppressed for too long. The wounds of the past demanded attention, and I had to face them head-on to find healing. Desperate for resolution, I sought therapy and unraveled the tangled threads of my family's history, gaining a deeper understanding and awareness that propelled me forward.

The path to freedom and redemption is still unfolding, and I am waiting with bated breath to embrace the possibilities that lie ahead. Join me as I probe deeper into the transformative process of generational curses and breaking these curses the Bible way, discovering the strength that lies within and embracing the power to create a legacy of hope and resilience for the generations to come. Together, we will unveil the secrets to rewriting your family's story and embarking on a journey toward liberation like no other.

Breaking Generational Curses From The Bible's Perspective

Generational curses, as mentioned in the Bible, refer to the negative patterns and consequences of sin that can pass down from one generation to another. These curses can affect families and individuals, creating cycles of hardship, bondage, and dysfunction. However, the Bible offers hope and guidance on how to break these generational curses and live in freedom and victory.

1. **Understanding Generational Curses:** The Bible teaches that sin has repercussions that can affect the future. We see examples of this in various scriptures, such as Exodus 20:5, which states that God *"punishes the children for the sin of the parents to the third and fourth generation."* This does not mean that God is unjust or punishes innocent children for their parents' sins, but it highlights the ripple effects of sin that linger in a family's lineage if not broken. Generational curses can manifest in different ways, such as addictions, unhealthy relationships, financial struggles, and chronic illnesses, among others.

2. **Identifying Generational Patterns:** To break generational curses, it is crucial to identify the negative patterns or sins that have been recurring in one's family history. This may require seeking wisdom from older family members, examining past traumas, and honestly assessing one's own life. Awareness is the first step toward healing and transformation.

3. **Repentance and Confession:** Breaking free from generational curses involves repentance and confession of sin, both personal and ancestral. Admitting our sins before God and asking for forgiveness is essential to receiving God's grace and cleansing. Nehemiah 1:6 says, "*I confess the sins we Israelites, including myself and my father's family, have committed against you.*"

4. **Embracing God's Grace and Forgiveness:** In Christ, we find redemption and forgiveness of sins. Ephesians 1:7 tells us, "*In him, we have redemption through his blood, the forgiveness of sins in accordance with the riches of God's grace.*" By accepting Jesus as our Lord and Savior, we are no longer under the condemnation of sin, and the power of generational curses is broken.

5. **Prayer and Spiritual Warfare:** Prayer is a powerful weapon in breaking generational curses. Engaging in spiritual warfare, we can renounce the authority of darkness over our lives and claim the victory that Christ already won for us. James 5:16 encourages us to confess our sins to each other and pray for each other so that we may be healed.

6. **Renewing the Mind with God's Word:** Transforming our minds with the truth of God's words is important in breaking free from generational patterns. Romans 12:2 advises, *"Do not conform to the pattern of this world, but be transformed by the renewing of your mind."* Meditating on scripture, prayer, and seeking godly counsel can help replace negative thought patterns with God's promises and principles.

Never underestimate a person who wants to see a change in their family lineage or be a cycle breaker. I am very passionate about this subject. Not only did I experience years of generational traumas, but I stood in the face of the ordeal and fought, saying, "This ends with me!" This is brave and powerful, but it comes at a significant cost.

I am the generational curse breaker, the one

God sent to destroy and dismantle the meaninglessness presented before me. The role was not easy because I had to break off some things that were like permanent daggers in me, my family members, and future generations.

I understood that I would be ridiculed and forsaken because I showed up and appeared differently. So, the past was brought up very often to attack and stop me, but I was determined to keep going. Breaking chains is not easy; it requires a lot of force and strength to undo the heaviness tied into years of bad teachings, unacceptable development, and stagnation, which were not mine to own. I caught hell for doing good, but I knew better than to let it deviate me from the given task ahead.

My dreams, visions, aspirations, and plans depended upon my willingness to act; I knew it was all about breaking the cycles and resetting the whole operation that was created to bury me. This special kind of weapon utilizes all of its functions and annihilates everything sent to destroy me and my family.

I had one job — to unknot everything that was done so that the whole nine yards afterward had a chance to thrive in wealth, health, power, respect, morality, and freedom. This assignment is now canceled over me and my immediate and extended family in Jesus' name!

Jesus has changed my life, and I will not make any apology for that. I have lost some friends along the way because I stand in my truth. Indeed, there is power, wonder-working power in the blood of the lamb. Just because it runs in the family doesn't mean it runs in your life; break that cycle now.

I can always run to Jesus; I love Him so much. He is so real to me, and my doubts are settled.

When your standard is high, you will lose some friends, which can be very hurtful, but know you will get new friends. Also, set boundaries and know that God is filtering your circle.

The story of my life and who I am today wasn't built overnight. I faced many battles. I had to pull myself out of dark places, insecurities, betrayal, and heartaches. I had to go through the crushing, pressing, grinding, pain, and tears to get here, and I give God all the glory. I will continue to be the best version of what God wants me to be. I am humbled. God gives us the choice to live a blessed life; all we have to do is make the correct choices.

Deuteronomy 30:19-20 says, *"This day I call the heavens and the earth as witnesses against you that I have set before life and death, blessings and curses. Now choose life, so that you and your children may live. And that you may love the Lord your God, listen to his voice, and hold fast to him. For the Lord is your life, and he will give you many years in the land he swore to give to your fathers, Abraham, Isaac, and Jacob."*

CHAPTER 4

Prayer for a Better Life

As an intercessor, prayer plays a pivotal role in my spiritual journey. Prayer, for me, is not just a practice but a habit and a deep-seated divine calling on my life, which means depending on God completely. Prayer is my priority; it is my life, and I am a living prayer. When I pray, there is a reaction from my inner self to the action of my thoughts, feelings, and attitudes. The answer to my prayer is in the prayer itself when it is prayed.

I consider myself a fool for Christ and can relate to the Apostle Paul in 1 Corinthians 4:10 (AMP).

"We are (regarded as) fools for Christ, but you are wise in Christ." Standing in the gap for others, lifting their needs, concerns, and aspirations is my privilege, joy, and the greatest conferment from Almighty God. My prayer involves continuous communication, daily petitions, listening, discerning, having compassion and empathy, faith, trust, consistency, persistence, thanksgiving, and studying God's word.

Prayer for a better life involves getting rid of thoughts that cause trouble in our minds: fear, hate, inferiority, and guilt. We dissolve them every day with prayer according to Proverbs 4:23 (NIV), *"Keep your heart with all vigilance, for from it flow the springs of life."* We can't afford to harbor hate, hostility, resentment, or jealousy because these emotions destroy us.

Prayer enables my spiritual growth, personal

transformation, and gives me a sense of purpose. For me, prayer is not about getting more but becoming more. I believe that unless something happens when I pray, there would be little point in praying. Prayer gives my life purpose and meaning. While I have served in many ministries, including the choir, praise and worship team, and the youth group, being an intercessor is my true calling. This ministry is the bridge between the needs of individuals; it is a path of selflessness, service, and an unfathomable spiritual connection.

Approach your prayer with the intention of experiencing the presence of God. Know that where the problem seems to be, God is already working there. Whatever it is that you are praying about or want to bring into your life, whatever condition or circumstance, prayer can change it. The result may be immediate or a sequence of unfoldment may begin, bringing about results in a natural development. Remember, the action of your prayer is taking place, and we must expect something to happen as a result of prayer.

Don't be embarrassed to talk out loud to God. He is not going to be upset, no matter what kind of prayer you pray. Don't worry about offending Him or how it is going to sound; learn to speak your words with pride, conviction, strength, faith, and love. When you speak your prayer verbally, it helps you keep track of where your own mind is going. The mind has a tendency to wander during prayer; order your mind to pay attention. The person who controls their mind controls their life; turn your mind Godward and fill it with God. Remove all superstitions from your prayer.

As born-again believers, prayer is not an option but a must. We are not given the choice to pray; it is important that we pray. When we pray daily, something extraordinary happens. The people of God have prayed from the earliest period in the history of mankind. Abraham, called the friend of God, prayed unto God habitually, thereby receiving extraordinary blessings.

Moses, though often referred to as "the servant of God," maintained a relationship and fellowship with Him. "*The Lord would speak to Moses face to face, as one speaks to a friend*" (Exodus 33:11). Through this privilege of prayer, Moses influenced many throughout history. The name of Moses is mentioned 804 times in the Bible. This special right was not reserved for selected or special friends of God; it is ours and yours. Prayer helps us secure the power and assistance of Omnipotence so that our lives achieve more than we would have achieved ordinarily.

Man becomes taller when he bends and kneels in prayer before God. The noblest activity that accomplishes the highest achievement is prayer. Each person becomes greater when in true communion with Almighty God. God's power in your life becomes stronger, and the power of evil becomes weaker.

In this unprincipled world – a dog-eat-dog situation – the world doesn't fight fair. However, we don't live to fight our battles that way, never have, and never will. Saints, contend for your prayer life. Pray and faint not. Living in this day and age, with the current pace of life, then you understand what this command means in the context of the "present day."

God does not evolve with culture; His word remains sure for every generation. The apostle Paul instructed the Thessalonians to *"pray without ceasing*" (1 Thessalonians 5:17). Prayer should be a believer's lifestyle, a conversation with God. Above all else, prayer is fellowshipping with the Father. It is not a mere spiritual tool to ask and receive answers from God.

All the manmade laws of the world cannot put an end to prayer; it's a life-sustaining river that cannot run dry, an ignited fire that no amount of water can put out. The very idea of forbidding prayer is laughable; you might as well command the lightning to stop and the thunder to be silent.

Prayer, after all, is the very breath of the soul; it's the secret to hanging on to God. Let me borrow this quote from Charles Spurgeon: "I would rather teach one man to pray than ten men to preach; let prayer be your priority." God can use you and me to answer prayer. No Christian can live a victorious life without praying; prayer works.

One giant of the Old Testament who knew about prayer was Daniel. He had an excellent spirit, was gifted with wisdom and knowledge, chosen for leadership, and, most importantly, disciplined in prayer (Daniel 6:4-9). A plot against Daniel was fabricated and initiated. Daniel's enemies testified to his integrity and character because he lived a truly blameless life. This was frustrating to his attackers, and their game plan sounds very much like the way politicians campaign against each other in today's society.

They were like, "All right, let's see what dirt we can dig up on this guy," but there was not a skeleton in Daniel's closet. Daniel's enemies, examining his life, found nothing on him, so they made something up. This should be expected treatment for born-again believers; we do not expect justice or equity from this world, yet we trust in a God who can defend us in all circumstances. Daniel was the object of attack because of his notability; even so, the devil directs special attacks on believers. These men could predict Daniel's behavior, and they had a right to. Can the world predict your behavior?

The world is a very poor critic of "My Christianity," but it is a very sufficient one of my conduct. They don't know the basics of the doctrine of worship with God, but they can tell a bad temper, selfishness, conceitedness, or dishonesty when they see it. I am not implying that Daniel was sinless, but that he was a man of integrity; his sins were inward sins of omission, not outward, which is the sin of commission. Daniel's enemies appealed to Darius' pride and his desire for a unified domain. The suggested mode of compelling every subject in the former Babylonian domain to acknowledge the authority of Persia seemed a statesmanlike measure that could contribute to the unification of the Middle and Near East. The time limit of one month seems reasonable when they claimed all the governors of the kingdom had agreed to such a decree to put Daniel in the Lion's Den. The great sin of Daniel's enemies is envy.

In Daniel 6:10-13 - Daniel's faithfulness to God causes him to be condemned to the Lion's Den. He was confronted with the test of loyalties; Daniel wanted to render unto Caesar things that rightfully belonged to Caesar (St Matthew 22:21), but he would not give to the government that which belonged to God alone. It might have seemed that Daniel was not playing it safe in his refusal to pray as was his custom, but the safest thing he could do was radically obey God.

It's not hard to see why people are men-pleasers; it seems as if people have the power to hire and fire us, to break our hearts, to slander us, to make our lives ordinarily miserable. The power to obey God and stand for Him comes from a settled understanding that God is Sovereign and in control of our lives.

Daniel simply prayed as was his custom; it would have been compromising to change in any direction, but he continued in the faithful ministry of prayer, which has characterized his long life. Daniel kneeled in prayer, so did Jesus in Luke 22:41; Stephen in Acts 7:60; Peter in Acts 9:40; Paul and the other leaders in the church in Acts 20:36 and Luke in Acts 21:5. Daniel kneeling facing Jerusalem was symbolic of his hope that someday the children of Israel would be able to return to this city of God.

Notice that Daniel prayed and gave thanks; our prayers should be an offering of thanksgiving. Isn't it the greatest of today's ingratitude? In verse 13, Daniel's enemies are coloring their report of the matter, but he intended no disrespect, only higher respect for his God. Indeed, he was an exceptional man. Brothers and Sisters, "Dare to be a Daniel by becoming a person of purpose, principle, purity, and prayer.

I propel you to Pray On:

- Pray about becoming a better person.
- Pray to experience the presence of God.
- Pray about developing your soul.
- Pray about the revelation of the spirit within you.
- Pray for those who despitefully use you.
- Pray when your prayer goes unanswered.
- Pray for your church family.
- Pray for your country.
- Pray for your family.

- Pray for the community you live in.
- Pray for your unsaved friends and families.
- Pray in good and bad times.
- Pray until something happens.
- Pray in supplication, fasting, and sackcloth.
- Pray at all times in every circumstance.
- Pray and faint not.
- Pray for the sick and shut-in.

CHAPTER 5

Rejection God's Favor

As I reminisced about the dark history of my past, reflecting on how I was ostracized, marginalized, isolated, and rejected because of my faith in God and my transformation. I was no longer the person who compromises, and this change didn't sit well with some people.

In those challenging times, I had to encourage myself when doubts assailed me. I had to be of good courage during moments when I looked in the mirror and was reminded that I didn't look like what I had been through. There were times when I felt like throwing in the towel, but I had to pick myself up and start all over again. In those moments, I knew unequivocally that God's favor in my life outweighed all the rejections I had ever endured, and what I went through qualified me for where I am now. My story produced the glory of God that everyone sees.

I believe that rejection is a universal human experience that transcends confines, cultures, and ages. It is a natural part of our journey through life, and although it often carries negative feelings, rejection takes various forms in our lives.

While the initial sting of rejection is undoubtedly painful, it is essential to recognize that it is not the end of the road but rather a fork in the path of life. One of the profound effects of rejection is its ability to foster emotional resilience. When faced with rejection, we are forced to confront our emotions, navigate disappointment, and find ways to heal. This process helps build emotional strength and enables us to handle future setbacks. It also teaches us that it is okay to feel vulnerable and that vulnerability can be a source of strength.

Rejection provides an opportunity for self-reflection, forcing us to evaluate our goals, desires, and actions. We may discover areas where we have fallen short and how we can improve, learn new skills, or develop a better understanding of ourselves. In this sense, rejection can be a catalyst for personal growth, pushing us to strive for excellence and pursue our passions with even greater determination.

Rejection can shape our character profoundly and teach us patience, perseverance, and the importance of humility. When we experience rejection, we learn to appreciate the value of hard work and determination, encouraging us to stay committed to our goals and convictions, even in the face of adversity.

Having experienced rejection many times myself, I have become more empathetic and compassionate towards others who face similar challenges. I developed a deeper understanding of the emotional toll rejection can take on a person and am more inclined to offer support and encouragement to those in need. This sense of empathy strengthens my connections with others and fosters a more compassionate society.

Remember, not every rejection is meant to harm you the way you think. There are times when God blocks others from you because they probably had bad intentions toward you. Remember, God takes care of His own. Never feel as if you aren't enough for the right people or job. Being rejected may mean that others see your potential and are threatened by it, attempting to hinder your progress.

Learn to be resilient, bouncing back from rejections that others thought would break you. Work on yourself by spending time with God and allowing Him to work on you. Avoid plotting revenge; this may seem right in the heat of anger, but carrying out vengeful deeds can lead to regret and guilt. Save yourself the trouble of bringing shame and more drama into your life over another person's actions. Also, avoid blaming yourself.

Do not search too deeply within yourself for mistakes you probably did not make, causing that person or place to reject you. Remain positive and hopeful for better times and situations ahead. Don't fight it. When rejected, either by people you love or in general, don't ask or wonder why. Burdening yourself with thoughts or feelings that you didn't do enough is neither healthy nor necessary. Take time alone if you have to and regain your composure.

Being rejected is very painful, and who better knew about rejection than Jesus? If we look at His life, we find a road map of how God has empowered each of us to respond to rejection. In Mark 6:1-13, we see where Jesus was rejected at Nazareth, His hometown. Dealing with rejection should always remind yourself that you are in the very same company as Jesus Christ.

First and foremost, seek God's favor rather than the favor of men. People may lift you up one day and throw you under the bus the next. It's very human to desire the approval of man; we seek approval from everyone, including parents, fellow church members, and peers. However, seeking God's approval is crucial because if God approves of us, no one else's approval matters. God's acceptance of you is much more important than man's approval.

It doesn't matter who has rejected you and offended you. Regardless of who they are, they will give an account to God concerning their treatment of you. It's almost impossible to go through life without feeling some sort of rejection. Most of us have had bad experiences that stayed with us for years. But if you seek God's favor by living the kind of life He created you to live, you can overcome everything else. "*Be of good cheer, I have overcome the world*" (John 16:33).

When people rejected Jesus, He didn't hang around desperately trying to make them accept Him. He knew that His Father was in control of the situation, and it was because of the anointing that scares the daylight out of Satan that others would be used to attack you, even people who are members of the very church you attend. How sad. Jesus didn't keep talking to those who rejected Him, and He didn't try to convince them to accept His message. If you notice, He left them alone and continued to go about His Father's business.

Jesus left because He had to be about His Father's business, and so He just left the message that He gave them. It was up to them to accept it or reject it. So, how do we deal with rejection? We go to God and get His instructions and guidance as to what we should do. It's as simple as that.

When you feel like you don't belong, go to God with your concerns because with Him, you are 100% welcome. In the above scripture, Jesus didn't allow rejection to stop Him from doing what God called Him to do. He sent the disciples two by two out into the villages to preach, teach, and heal.

In Mark 6:11, Jesus even tells His disciples, "*If any place will not welcome you and they refuse to hear you, as you leave, shake off the dust that is on your feet as a testimony against them.*" What exactly did Jesus mean? I believe He meant for them not to allow their egos to get in the way, not to become angry or bitter, and not to keep trying to convince people to accept them. Most of the time, when others reject us, it is done to feed their self-image.

Rejection is very dangerous; it makes you feel all alone. If you allow it to fester, if you allow it to attach itself to you, you allow the very people who reject you to control you as well. And I don't know about you, but the only one I will allow to have control of my life is God Himself. If you have the favor of God and the anointing, people may throw things at you that you don't want.

People want what you have. The story of Joseph

is a perfect example in Genesis 37, which starts with jealousy and a dream. Joseph's brothers hated him so much that they plotted to kill him. This indeed is about family rejection, "*Come now, let us kill him and throw him into one of the pits. Then we will say that a fierce animal has devoured him, and we will see what will become of his dreams*" Genesis 37:20 (ESV).

Thankfully, relatively better sense prevailed, and they ended up selling him into slavery in Egypt instead. Unfortunately, Joseph spent the next several years as a slave, and then in prison after he was falsely accused of a crime. He was rejected again, this time by the master whom he had served faithfully. "*And Joseph's master took him and put him into prison, the place where the King's prisoners were confined, and he was there in prison*" Genesis 39:20 (ESV). Everyone failed Joseph, but the Lord didn't reject or abandon Joseph. "But the Lord was with

Joseph in the prison and showed him his faithful love. And the Lord made Joseph a favorite with the prison warden" Genesis 39:21 (NLT).

Being rejected doesn't have to dictate your feelings or your actions. You can choose to be faithful in any situation, no matter how bad it may be. God has your back, just like Joseph, so do your best despite rejection. *"The warden had no more worries because Joseph took care of everything. The Lord was with him and caused everything he did to succeed"* Genesis 39:23 (NLT). I love Genesis 50:20 (ESV): "As for you, you meant evil against me, but God meant it for good, to bring it about that many people should be kept alive, as they are today."

CHAPTER 6

The Resplendent Beauty of a Late Bloomer

In a world that often celebrates early achievements and rapid success, the beauty of a late bloomer stands as a validation of the wonderful and changeable nature of life, like a radiant flower on the hillside waiting to be discovered. A late bloomer possesses a unique lure that captivates hearts and inspires souls. My journey, though filled with challenges and uncertainties, unfolds with grace, resilience, and an unbendable spirit.

The steps into the intriguing play in my life

oftentimes look like that of a puzzling preface. I may have spent my early years in the shadows, unseen by the spotlight that decorates the achievements of my peers. But hidden beneath the surface lies a world of untapped potential and dormant dreams patiently awaiting the moment to shine.

It is during this period of quiet growth that I gathered the heart of life's experiences like precious drops of morning dew on flowers. I observed, learned, and internalized the world around me, slowly nurturing my passions and talents, and sometimes asking God how long. In the process, I developed an acute sense of compassion and understanding of the struggles and aspirations of others who may have also felt overlooked.

As time passes and the seasons of life change, my journey begins to take a remarkable turn. Just like the first rays of sunshine kissing the earth, a spark of inspiration ignites within me. With newfound clarity, I set out on a path of self-reflection, unafraid to explore uncharted territories and redefine my purpose.

This bird's eye view began when I lost my good-paying job of 14 years and was devastated. After countless job applications to no avail and wallowing in hopelessness, I asked God what step I should take and what move to make. In the first quarter of 2017, standing over my kitchen sink and doing the dishes, I heard the Holy Spirit in an audible voice giving the command "GO," according to (St. Matthew 28:19-20).

After this prophetic word, I also got the confirmation at a fasting and prayer service, so I decided to attend Bible school in the same year. However, I was not gainfully employed and didn't see how the school fees would be paid, even though others discouraged me from going and urged me to look for a job instead. I was resolute to be obedient to the Holy Spirit.

I am forever grateful to God for the opportunity to search the scriptures, and trust me we did. My prayer life went to another level. One of the best decisions I have ever made in my life. Embracing the concept of being a late bloomer took on a new and profound meaning for me. I learned much more than my many years as a Christian. God showed up regarding my school fees; to this day, it baffles me. Before graduation, everything was "Paid in Full." I even started a business during this time, supplying students with sweet treats that sold off most days before class and ordering for the following day.

The core memories are still so vivid that I cannot wrap my natural mind around them, along with many other testimonies of how God provided for me during this time. I finished school with graduate credits and the highest grades I have ever received in any exams, and I am ready to go to the next level. I have found my passion, and my odyssey as an author became real.

God doesn't call the qualified; He qualifies the called (1 Corinthians 2:1-5). As a late bloomer, I understand that slow and steady wins the race, and life is a marathon, not a sprint. I may have to struggle, fight, and even get knocked back, but I will persist.

I've learned to fully appreciate my achievements when earned honestly. Sometimes, the road to success is filled with detours, but these can be the most valuable instructive periods of the journey. I also know there is no shame in failure, and I can strive. It's not failure that defines me, but the moment I get back up and try again.

I've realized that I don't have to torture myself with an unrealistic timeline and should not close myself off from opportunities that come late in life. While many may stop expanding their horizons, one can still achieve in old age and doesn't have to settle. This scripture came to mind (Haggai 2:9), which talks about how the glory of the latter day will be greater than the glory of the former day.

This means that what God did for my parents and grandparents, what previous generations have experienced in terms of blessings and favor, was good, but God is a God of increase. He has greater things in store for me, and nothing compares to what He is about to do in my life.

I don't have to settle until I find my true passion. In the company of those great individuals who don't achieve early, I should feel proud to be a late bloomer. This scripture speaks loudly to me (St.

Matthew 20:16), *"So the last will be first, and the first last."* This statement is about reversals; God doesn't work the way the world works. The Kingdom of God is upended compared to the rules of men. It is not fair according to world standards that those who enter last end up on equal footing with those who entered first. With God, generosity comes before fairness.

In Matthew 22:14, *"For many are called, but few are chosen."* The statement above is not a paradox of the first but a qualification. This too relies on the reversal that becomes evident when comparing the Kingdom of God with the Kingdom of men. In today's world, bigger is considered better, and more is seen as best. God calls and invites everyone to participate with Him. In all that is going on in the world, every person plays a part, but this is God's way of working. He often selects a few individuals for special purposes and tasks. And what are these special purposes and tasks for which God chooses some? To serve, suffer, and die. God's "choosing" is not a choice of honor, position, and power, but of suffering and service.

Jesus is teaching that God is generous to all, and while all are called to serve Him, true service to God is not an easy thing to bear, which is why most don't want it. Yet God does choose some to serve Him in these difficult ways. In Matthew 20:17-19, Jesus shows what it means to be chosen by God, for Jesus Himself has been chosen. To be betrayed and condemned to death. He will be given over to the Gentiles, mocked, beaten, and crucified. This is not usually what people think of when they speak of being "chosen" by God. Someone had to pay the price, and He chooses only those who are willing to walk that hard road. If we let Him, He will turn our world right around for us so that we can see the truth and beauty that is God's Kingdom. But it will not come without pain, hardship, and a complete reversal of our worldly value system.

Wherever you find yourself, as an early achiever or late achiever, over-achiever, under-achiever, or non-achiever, whether it is your dream to go to college, Bible school, learn a skill, or become an author, God will fulfill every promise to you. God is not impartial, and He does not give preferential treatment; He is God all by Himself, according to Acts 10:34 (NIV). Then Peter began to speak: "*I now realize how true it is that God shows no favoritism.*" You are chosen, and your God-given purpose will be fulfilled.

CHAPTER 7

The Bible God's Word

The Bible, God's word, is my lifeline. It is the air I breathe, my compass, the wind beneath my wings, my rock, my source. It speaks peace to my soul, heals, corrects, strengthens, and transforms me into a better person

I can confidently say that studying the Bible, God's Word, has played an integral part in my born-again experience. In my regular devotions, meditations, and reflections, there are many precious promises that I have held close to my heart over the years. These promises from God are timely, and the Holy Spirit is always there to console me Jeremiah 1:12 (NLT).

I am still excited and enthusiastic about studying the Bible. This experience is incomparable; it shifts my focus from the fleshy desires of this world. Many times, I have had to declare God's word over my life by feeding my faith and starving my fear. The phrase "*If God said it, I believe it, and that settles it*" Ezekiel 12:25 (KJV) says it all. Be definite in believing what God's word says. Doubt none of His words, allow no shadows over it—not maybe—let it settle in your mind.

In Psalm 119:89 (KJV), it is declared, "*Forever, O Lord, thy word is settled in heaven.*" How long? For time and eternity. Permanently, the word of God is settled in heaven. This means the words are settled for us here on earth too. God has said it; all we have to do is believe it, and that settles it. So, we can use the promises of His word to receive anything and everything needed. The Holy Spirit works around the clock trying to get you and me to settle the word of God in our minds and spirits so that we can go and do His work here on earth. We will not make great workers for God if we do not settle in our hearts the will of God and the greatness and promises of God for us. Believe in His will for your life.

I distinctly remember my earlier years in the country living with my grandparents. Every night before bedtime, they asked me to read Psalm 27. At that time, I just read because I wanted to obey them and didn't think of the significance. After I got saved, I realized that it was a seed planted in the ground.

Reflecting on it now, I can know that God had His hand on me from my childhood, and this particular Psalm has been nothing short of an inspiration for me. I feel nostalgic because this time was one of the best times I had in the country. Then I would beg to ask, why me? And now I can answer, why not me?

John 15:16 (AMP) says it perfectly, "*You have not chosen me, but I have chosen you and I have appointed, placed, and purposefully planted you, so that you would go and bear fruit and keep on bearing, and that your fruit will remain and be lasting, so whatever you ask of the Father in my name (as my representative), He may give to you.*"

The word of God can bring you and me into the proper perspective of all God says we are, all He says we can do, and all that He says we can become because we are connected to Him. Throughout the years, I have gleaned so many lessons from Psalm 27. It's a psalm that declares God's faithfulness.

King David wrote about his confidence and trust in God; it is such a wonderful passage that allows us to see Divine providence and protection of His people through this poetic and beautiful writing of King David. It is packed with profound meaning and deep insights into the nature of God and how His people can trust Him in times of need.

Some lessons I have learned from Psalm 27: I must not be afraid, God is my light, God is my salvation, God is my strength, God is my refuge, and my ultimate desire is to serve Him.

Let's look more deeply at the Bible, it is the infallible word of God. It's perfect pure, flawless, impeccable, sure, clean, eternal, and a mirror, hammer, fire, lamp, food, and seed. It convicts, regenerates, purges, cleanses, reveals, illuminates, and nourishes the heart, see these scripture references. 2 Tim. 3:16-17, 2 Peter 1:19-21, Psalm

19:7-9 and Revelation 22:18-19. The Bible is the final authority and the last court of appeal in matters about Christian conduct and lifestyle and is not subject to changing culture and circumstances.

I want to feature the mirror in this section. The word of God is like a mirror that reveals to us the very feelings and intents of our hearts. God's word is living and active, sharper than any two-edged sword, piercing to the division of soul and of spirit, of joints and marrow, and discerning the thoughts and intentions of the hearts.

Hebrews 4:12. The word of God – mirror shows us our ugly, self-centered attitudes. It exposes our pride and confronts our contempt for others, our lack of compassion, our sinful anger, and our bad speech. It uncovers our deception greed, and lust. But if we just take a glance at the word once in a while without doing anything to address the problems that it reveals, it won't do us any good.

The purpose of the mirror is to show what we look like, so we can improve ourselves. It is the examiner of what is seen, not by us, but by others. It is the same with the Bible. God's word examines and gives us the information to "comb" the hair of our faith, to make us worthy of going out in public, and to be practical and appealing to others. The Bible helps us to see ourselves so we can fix, with the spirit of empowerment what needs your attention and improvement.

James 1:23 states, "*If anyone is a hearer of the word and not a doer, he is like a man who looks intently at his natural face in the mirror.*" For a person to behold their reflection, and see the imperfections, one had to examine himself or herself very intently. What James is showing here is that a hearer is like a man who goes to the mirror and examines himself.

He does not do so with care and concern, in great detail because that is the only way one can get a true perspective of what the mirror is reflecting. However, upon examining himself, the hearer turns away without regard for what he just saw in the mirror. He does not take the time to fix the blemishes or imperfections and instead continues as he was. In this manner, he has deceived himself into thinking that he is better than he is. In verse 25, James gives the opposite example, explaining that a person who examines the law (which is God's word) and remains in it is a doer.

The doer will not forget the word but rather act upon it and apply it to his or her life. The doer uses God's word as the basis for living, looking keenly into it as the mirror. The word of God then becomes the mirror in which one is to examine himself. The word 'keenly' suggests that the person is looking at it deeply, studying it to see what God's law says, in Psalms 19:7 (KJV).

The law is the Lord is perfect, converting the soul: the testimony of the Lord is sure, making wise the simple. So that one can conform to it. The call here is for every person to examine himself or herself in the mirror of God's word, comparing what it says to what your life acts finding a reflection of your true character, and seeking thus, to change the image being reflected of himself into the image of Christ.

Believers should be using God's word as their mirror. As a mirror, allow it to reflect an image of who you truly are. When it shows you your gifts, use them. I must say writing this topic gives me the 'Revelation Knowledge' just from verse 23. When the mirror shows you what you are doing wrong, recognize and change it. When it shows you how you can live in the power of Christ, live in it.

This should be a tool for you to use to examine your life, but it must be done truthfully. One cannot examine themselves in God's word and then not respond. Let your time of daily devotion be an opportunity to do just that, let it be a time of examining yourself in the mirror of God's word.

Therefore, be in the word more and seek it, read it, learn it, meditate on it, apply it, and teach it. Let the Word of God richly dwell in your life and let it be reflected in our lives.

I just love this quote by Charles Spurgeon: "The more you read the Bible, and the more you meditate on it you will be astonished by it."

As I complete this chapter, I have realized that to be effective in prayer, one has to pray from the Bible.

CHAPTER 8

Unshakable Faith

Traveling on this luxurious express bus on this sunny Saturday morning, heading into the second city of this beautiful island of Jamaica with my husband. I embarked on a privileged mission to lead the opening prayer at my friend's celebration party.

As I gazed upon the picturesque lush green vegetation, shading the area from the sun and keeping it cool, a sense of joyful gladness filled the air. The mountaintop, the valley, the straight and bent roads—all unfolded before me. I felt the elevation of the vehicle going uphill, inhaling the fresh, clean air, and contemplating the marvelous movements of God. For days, I struggled with a mental block, unable to write. However, as clarity dawned, I took out my writing pad and began penning this chapter.

Reflecting on my journey by faith in Christ Jesus, I realized it was a long but worthwhile path. God brought me into the desired haven of rest and unshakable faith. Wrestling with the desire to control everything, I learned that unshakable faith is not built overnight; it took years in my Christian walk to establish this foundation.

I prayed, asking God to step forward into whatever my unique calling required each day. Sometimes, this meant acting with integrity or 'walking' my talk, even if others were disappointed or rejected my godly decision. Faced with spiritual crossroads, I reminded myself that I belonged to Jesus.

My life was marked by failures, doubts, fears, anxieties, and mistakes. Yet, when I entered that secret place, knelt before God in prayer and supplication, and listened carefully to the Holy Spirit—the Word of God—I was amazed every time. Remember, God speaks to us through His written words.

Whatever you hear, whether a phrase, idiom, one word, many words, a hymn, or a song, research it. Don't be in a hurry; you might miss what He is saying to you. When I needed direction or instruction, perhaps in confusion or misunderstanding, all I had to do was ask, and the answer was loud and clear Proverbs 3:5-6 (MSG).

Trust God from the bottom of your heart; don't try to figure out everything on your own.

Listen for God's voice in everything you do, everywhere you go; He is the one who will keep you on track.

Ironically, when I sent this manuscript for review in July 2023, the response was not favorable. Things didn't go as planned, and I had to rewrite this book. Discouragement set in because I thought it was perfect. I decided not to continue writing, feeling stuck after all the hard work. I had given my manuscript to an editor before and haven't received a reply to this day. I disliked the idea of starting over. One can imagine the disappointment, and I said, 'Lord, you gave me this book; where do I go from here?' I heard the Holy Spirit say, "Now, Faith" (Hebrews 11:1).

Also, you are going to need unshakable faith on this second lap. I had to go back to the drawing board and do a complete study on this topic, and that's how God moves. It may be frustrating at times, but He knows what is best for us; we just have to listen to His voice and be obedient. I must say, after doing my study, I developed dogged faith and was ready for the remaining challenges, which included changing the title and topics, rearranging the chapters, removing and building. I was pleasantly surprised by how failure never has the sting I imagine.

I know that failure is one of those things that many of us shy away from, and for obvious reasons. It can be scary and not an easy pill to swallow. After all, who wants to put in all the work, go for this big goal, and fail? I want to tell you from my own experience that failure is one of the best things that could ever happen to me. It allowed me to start over, changed me, and I learned that true success is not in finishing this book in record time or being perfect; it is about first having patience, joy, peace, love, and passion for what I do. Embracing my failure, knowing that it's going to be a part of my journey, and committing to failing forward.

Proverbs 24:10 says, *"If you faint in the day of adversity, your strength is small."* In the Bible, great men and women did not quit; they were overcomers. They ignored difficulties, resisted tiredness, and fought opposition. They understood that negative events would come, so they prepared for them and fought through them. Don't quit when the going gets tough; let God be true in your life always.

Unshakeable faith means never wavering or faltering in our belief in God's character. It is easy to trust God when things are good in our lives. But if you only claim to believe when things are fine, then your faith is fragile. It is in the hard times, in times of trouble, that you get to realize if your faith is truly solid or not. The worth of your faith is never known in peace, but only in difficult times. Whatever you believe about God, the world, and yourself will be challenged by the circumstances in which you find yourself. Is your faith evident during difficulties? It will be after the trials have tested you that you know whether your faith is unshakable or not.

Unshakable faith is very important because your enemy, Satan, is bent on deceiving us into abandoning our path, just as he did in the Garden of Eden. Satan wants you to believe that your purpose doesn't matter, that your calling isn't from God, and that your time is better spent in more self-centered pursuits. Don't listen to the negative voice of Satan. Listen to God's words, and don't quit; you got this.

All of us as Christians face times when we must make difficult decisions to affirm our convictions. These crisis moments help us assess the level of witnesses who see us face these challenges and who learn from our example. Every one of us is going to face something in our life that will shake our faith to its foundation: loss, doubt, disappointment, betrayal, and discouragement.

Are we in the business of building up our faith to its greatest strength as we prepare for the day we need it most? Would your faith today sustain you through a significant trial? The higher level of unshakable faith rests in what God has said and is saying; you will experience the low before the high—no shaking, it is working

Many people have already lost family, friends, jobs, and other life opportunities because of their faith in God and their commitment to His laws.

Those of us who are dedicated Christians undertook our devotion with a willingness to sacrifice everything

The Bible story of Daniel assimilates the narrative of Shadrach, Meshach, and Abednego. When we compare the circumstances of the book of Daniel with the reality of our own lives, it is striking for these men to have trusted in the unseen God with such unshakable faith that they were willing to be thrown into a fiery furnace (Daniel 3:2-29) to honor God.

It can be uncomfortable to dwell on the potential outcomes of this frightening time in our world today. However, by loving God and having a strong relationship with Him, we will be given all the resources in crisis to step out in real faith, knowing that the God whom we trust will raise us. One can ask the question: What makes a great professional athlete outstanding? It's the one who endures to the end no matter the mountain there is to face. In the Bible, people like Noah, Moses, Abraham, Peter, and Paul were all great men who lived ordinary lives yet became extraordinary. They didn't live for themselves but for the purpose and will of their Father because of the trust they placed in God.

Matthew 16:24 says, "*Then Jesus said to his disciples, if any man will come after me, let him deny himself, and take up his cross, and follow me.*" Unshakable faith is a faith that has total trust and reliance on God no matter the situation. It's like when an earthquake strikes in your life—no matter the magnitude of the quake, you are left unmoved. Perhaps shaken, but not moved or broken. Unshakable faith points others toward God and causes them to praise Him.

Through small acts of faithful obedience, let us consider our obedience to God in the everyday challenges we face so that God can build us on a truly unshakable foundation of faith. May God give us the confidence, strength, and genuine faith to follow Jesus until the end.

CHAPTER 9

When the Time is Right

Throughout my life, I have encountered countless moments when I had to make decisions, whether big or small, take action, or embark on new journeys. Oftentimes, the question that weighs heavily on me is, 'When is the right time?' As I reflect on my high noon, I have come to recognize that determining when the time is right is a deeply personal matter, motivated by my unique circumstances and aspirations.

For me, the notion of 'the right time' is intrinsically tied to self-awareness; it begins with an understanding of oneself, one's goals, values, and dreams. When I am in tune with my innermost desires, I will better gauge when an opportunity aligns with my vision for the future. This self-awareness acts as a compass, guiding me toward making decisions that resonate most with my authentic self.

Timing often plays a crucial role in the pursuit of our goals. There are moments when I must exercise patience and allow circumstances to unfold naturally. In these instances, the right time means waiting for the right conditions to manifest. As I've learned, patience can be a virtue, for it allows us to prepare and grow, ensuring that when we do seize an opportunity, we are better equipped to make the most of it. However, there are also occasions when seizing the moment becomes of prime importance. Opportunities can be fleeting, and if I hesitate too long, they may slip through my fingers.

Recognizing when to take action is a delicate balance between being well-prepared and having the courage to leap into the unknown. It's about trusting God and listening to His voice that urges you to move forward, even if it means taking risks. Moreover, the right time can be profoundly influenced by external factors; it's essential to be aware of the world around us, including economic conditions and societal shifts. These external forces can greatly impact the feasibility and outcome of our decisions. Adapting to changing circumstances and seizing opportunities when they align with the greater context can be a defining factor in our personal and professional journeys.

In my life, there have been junctures when I hesitated, waiting for the 'perfect' time, only to realize that perfection is elusive. Writing this book is a perfect example. I've also experienced the exhilaration of taking a leap of faith when my instincts told me it was the right time, and these moments have often led to personal growth, success, and the creation of the life I envisioned.

The Bible says in Isaiah 60:22b, *"At the right time, I, the Lord, will make it happen."* God is making things happen for you, even when you don't see it with your naked eyes, even when you can't feel it, even if it is not evident... God is working on your prayers 'In his time' 2 Peter 3:8 (NIV), *"But do not forget this one thing, dear friends: with the Lord, a day is like a thousand years, and a thousand years are like a day."* God moves in His timing, not yours. He is never late, but He is usually not early either. He is often the God of the midnight hour. Sometimes He waits until the last second before He gives you what you need; this is so true, and I have experienced this so many times.

Before He intervenes on your behalf, He has to be sure you are not going to take matters into your own hands and do something out of His perfect timing. We must all learn to trust God's timing. But first, self and your spirit of independence must be broken so that God is free to work His will in your life and circumstances.

I know sometimes the waiting period seems so long, and life has thrown you several curveballs, knocking you down with hard times, and you don't have any fight in you left. But remember, 'A setback is nothing but a setup for a comeback.' The wisdom in these words can help lift you out of your rock bottom in life and put you on the path to victory. Despite the adversities, refuse to cower in the face of hardships; turn your trials into triumphs, your problems into possibilities, and your setbacks into a comeback.

I hear The Holy Spirit saying this is your season to reap what you have sown, and Genesis 8:22 (NIV) said it perfectly, "*As long as the earth endures, seedtime and harvest, cold and heat, summer and winter, day and night will never cease.*" What have you sown? What dreams, visions, and desires has the Lord placed in your heart? Where there is no vision, the people perish - (Proverbs 29:18), but our God has given us His visions, desires, and dreams.

As we seek to know Him more each day, they become clearer; acceleration, multiplication, and instant harvest are manifesting as unexpected sources of passive income, new business opportunities, and new partnerships are coming to help bring your vision out into the natural. I strongly believe this word is for everyone reading this book. 'Is there anything too hard for me?'

(Jeremiah 32:27b). You shall succeed in all your endeavors in Jesus' Name.

May God's goodness surround you, and His favor be upon you, and may wisdom work on my behalf. God's name shall be glorified in all the earth through your life. What He calls blessed can never be taken away. You are not forgotten; your sacrifices will not be in vain. Just like Job's patience is perfecting your faith, ready the storehouses, and prepare for the harvest.

It shall exceed your dreams and visions. It is pouring out now; expect it! Receive it! There is no end to your heavenly provision. This shall be a quick one. Open your hands and open your heart, for God is releasing blessings upon blessings and grace upon grace. His kingdom has no end; He is your provider, and He will never forsake His children. "*God is not a man that should lie*" (Numbers

23:19a). He is faithful.

He will fulfill every promise to you, for there is work to be done and ground yet to be tilled. Be ready for God's glory. 'What's that in your hand?' (Exodus 4:2b). When God looks at your hands, He sees unlimited potential for blessings, miracles, and prosperity. We already have that authority as believers! See John 3:35. It's your time for greatness; reap all that you have sown Ephesians 3:20 (KJV), "*Now unto him that is able to do exceedingly abundantly above all that we ask or think according to the power that worketh in us.*" Whether you are an intercessor or minister, God's favor and blessing will be yours. It is reaping time.

Now is a good time. If you don't know Jesus as your Lord and Savior, right now is your time to answer the call. There is never a good or a bad time; just come as you are and hear the Spirit's call. No matter what you have done in your past, He will accept you with open arms. In the Gospel of John 6:37b (KJV), "*Whosoever comes to him, he will not cast them away.*" So choose Jesus right now before it is too late. Repeat this sinners prayer below, find yourself a Bible-believing church and just tell them you have accepted Jesus as your personal Savior. Trust me; you will not regret this decision.

Lord Jesus, I repent of my sins and surrender my life. Wash me clean. I believe that Jesus Christ is the Son of God, that He died on the cross for my sins, and rose again on the third day for my victory. I believe in my heart and confess with my mouth that Jesus is my Savior and Lord. Amen!

God makes all things beautiful in His time. This is my prayer, and it should be yours also: "Lord, please show me every day as you teach me your way.

Father, I give my life to you. May each prayer I pray and each song I sing, each sermon I preach be to you a lovely thing 'in your time.'"

God's timing is perfect, and He has the final say Ecclesiastes 3:14 (MSG), *"I've also concluded that whatever God does, that's the way it's going to be, always."* No addition, no subtraction. God did it, and that's it. That's so we'll quit asking questions and simply worship in holy fear.

CHAPTER 10

You Are Enough – Men

In this final chapter, I want to encourage men: 'You are enough.' Firstly, acknowledge that being a man is not defined solely by external attributes or traditional roles. Your worth is not determined by the ability to conform to the right ideals of masculinity. Instead, embrace your uniqueness, understand your emotions, and learn to be comfortable with vulnerability.

Embracing vulnerability does not mean losing strength; rather, it demonstrates a sincere toughness of character. It takes courage to acknowledge your weaknesses, express feelings, and seek help when needed. This authenticity allows you to connect more deeply with yourself and others, fostering healthier relationships and promoting good health.

Men, you are enough. This also means rejecting the harmful notion that success and achievement are the only markers of a man's worth. Society often pressures men to constantly strive for more, equating their value with external accomplishment. However, it's essential to recognize that indwelling worth is not tied to your job title, income, or material possessions. Men are valuable simply because of who they are as individuals, irrespective of their achievements.

Moreover, embracing the idea that 'You are enough' encourages self-compassion. At times, men can be particularly hard on themselves, expecting perfection in various aspects of life. However, understanding that it's okay to make mistakes, to learn, and to grow allows them to develop healthier self-images. They can also acknowledge their imperfections without feeling diminished by them.

Ultimately, 'You are enough' can be a reminder to men that they do not need to conform to external standards or suppress their true selves to fit into a narrow definition of masculinity. Your value lies in authenticity, capacity, understanding, and the ability to connect with others on a deeper level. Men, by embracing your vulnerabilities, not only do you become better partners, friends, and fathers but also more fulfilled individuals.

'You are enough' is a powerful mantra that encourages men to be their true selves, disregard harmful stereotypes, and embrace their vulnerabilities. Men, your worth must be inherent and not dependent on conforming to external expectations. By living authentically and allowing yourself to be vulnerable, you can break free from the limitations of societal pressures and live the God-kind of life.

Isaiah 49:16a (ESV) Says perfectly, *"Behold I have engraved you on the palms of my hands."* God is your maker, so He has the blueprint of how you should function the best way is to look at the manual which is the word of God that tells you who you are. Men you have to find God's dream and vision for your life. But the ultimate is knowing God your creator. You are a rare breed, irreplaceable, undeniable, and completely God's handmade.

In a world filled with expectations and pressures, it's easy for men to feel overwhelmed and uncertain about their worth, society often presents a skewed image of what it means to be a man, emphasizing strength, success, and unyielding confidence. But the truth is God made each man unique and possesses inherent value beyond these societal constructs.

Men whether you are teenagers, young adults, middle-aged, or senior citizens, might have great abilities, or disabilities, be marginalized or esteemed, educated or uneducated, no matter where you are in this life. Commit yourself to the task ahead, men God created you to multiply, start a men's group, sing in the choir, be a mentor for the boys in your community be a Sunday school teacher, keep on moving, and help a brother or sister in need, be the voice for the voiceless.

Pray for boldness and courage for the job at hand, stop looking back. When we are committed to God He will see us through. God made men to rule, accept the call, and take their rightful place in the Kingdom of God.

Remember, being enough as a man is not a destination but a continuous journey of self-discovery, growth, and self-respect, men you can do this. Envelop your uniqueness, and standards, re-evaluate success at God's' timetable, challenge society's expectations, nurture meaningful relationships, and practice self-compassion.

By doing so, you will discover the true value and worth that resides within and around you. Know that you are made in God's image, you are special and you have the power to shape your narrative and embrace the incredible person you are with God's help. Keep your head up high and remember that God gives his hardest battles to his strongest soldiers.

Men, here are some key points to remember:

1. **Embrace Your Individuality:** You are a distinct individual with your own set of talents, strengths, and weaknesses. Take advantage of the qualities that make you unique, as they contribute to your personal growth and impact on the world.

2. **Define Your Own Success:** Success means different things to diverse people. It is important to define what success means to you personally and not rely solely on societal benchmarks. Whether it's pursuing a passion, maintaining meaningful relationships, or making a positive difference, focus on what truly matters to you.

3. **Embrace Vulnerability:** Society often expects men to be strong and invulnerable,

but it's okay to show vulnerability and ask for support when needed. Emotional well-being is just as important as physical strength. Seek a healthy outlet to express your feelings, whether through exercise, trusted friends, therapy, or creative outlets.

4. **Cultivate Authentic Relationships:** Building genuine connections with others is vital for personal well-being. Surround yourself with people who accept you for who you are, not for what you have or can give. Seek friendships and partnerships that value open communication, empathy, and mutual support.

5. **Practice Self-Compassion:** Treat yourself with kindness, understanding, and forgiveness. Accept that you are human and bound to make mistakes. Practice self-care,

including grooming, and prioritize your well-being.

As I bring down the curtain on this book, I see where God is moving me from glory to glory. I started seeing more answered prayers like never before and was able to meet every disappointment with God's appointment.

I see where God strategically and chronologically brought me through a series of events and experiences, giving me these topics and contents in bits and pieces—sometimes in church, before or after prayer, in the supermarket, while walking, and even in the middle of the night. It truly amazes me how God works. He is good, omnipotent, ageless, timeless, boundless, notable, and everything He does is saturated with grace.

God reminds me that I owe Him everything. I am frail, helpless, and nothing without Him. I never want Him to take His hands off me.

When my mother passed away in February 2022, and I didn't get to talk to her during her last days on earth, He comforted me. The times I didn't fit into the crowd and also stuck out as one who 'didn't belong with the crowd,' I felt like an outcast. I was nobody when Jesus found me. I will choose Jesus again and again.

My Journey For God's Glory has been very fulfilling. Everything you go through is for a reason; I must be glorified in you (1 Corinthians 6:20). So my prayer is, Lord, I offer my life to You—everything I went through, use it for Your glory.

Amen!

References

1. Permission was granted by Deeper Life School of Evangelism to use materials
2. Search the Scriptures booklets
3. Bible Doctrines Abridged Edition
4. A short excerpt from the book "Live it Up" by Donald Curtis
5. Reasons to be glad you are a late bloomer: Huff. post by Abigail Williams, 2016
6. Faithwriters.com – "Be a Late Bloomer"
7. The Bible Handbook Series
8. Compact Bible Dictionary
9. Ellicott's Bible Commentary of English

Reader

10. W.E. Vine's Expository Dictionary Old Testament & New Testament

11. https://static1.squarespace.com "Unshakable Faith"

12. WordPress.com

13. The Theology of Work Bible Commentary

14. My Personal Journal since 1996

QUOTES BY

Mark Twain

Charles Spurgeon

Made in the USA
Columbia, SC
16 August 2024

40080111R00081